Nichola Fletcher has written a number of award-winning cookery books, including *Charlemagne's Tablecloth*, *Nichola Fletcher's Ultimate Venison Cookery*, *Caviar; A Global History* and *The Meat Cookbook*. She and her husband started Britain's first deer farm in 1973, and Nichola has devoted her life since then to helping people to appreciate, understand and cook venison (both wild and farmed) as well as other game meats. She was honoured with an MBE in 2014 for her work for the venison industry.

The
Venison
Bible

Nichola Fletcher

Illustrated by Bob Dewar

BIRLINN

For Harriet and Clara – small but perfectly formed,
like this wee book

First published in 2015 by
Birlinn Limited
West Newington House
10 Newington Road
Edinburgh
EH9 1QS

www.birlinn.co.uk

Copyright © Nichola Fletcher 2015
Artwork copyright © Bob Dewar 2015

ISBN: 978 1 78027 282 5

British Library Cataloguing-in-Publication Data
A catalogue record for this book is available
from the British Library

Designed and typeset by Mark Blackadder

Printed and bound by Gutenberg Press Ltd, Malta

Contents

Venison treasure chest

Roasting venison

Slow-cooking venison

What to serve with venison

ROE DEER BUCK ·· QUARTER SIZE OF RED DEER · WOODLAND ·

Introduction

A deer for all seasons

During the 40 or so years I have been working with venison I have had the satisfaction of seeing it emerge from being virtually unknown and almost feared by cooks, to becoming one of the most popular speciality meats. Its delicious flavour is not its only appeal – venison's healthy properties are now well understood, and at last this refreshing, low-fat meat is available to buy and eat all year round instead of being confined to the winter months.

But it is still a bit more complicated than other meat because of two things: 'venison' can come from any one of several different deer species, the largest of which can be up to ten times as big as the smallest. This affects the size of the cuts and how it is butchered; on top of that, there is the age difference between farmed venison (all young) and wild deer, which varies but is generally older when shot. The condition of wild deer also varies. Fortunately, now that all venison is handled so much better than when I first encountered it, its true flavour can now be properly appreciated.

Red deer, undoubtedly Scotland's most iconic animal,

are Britain's largest native land-mammal. They are mostly found in the Scottish Highlands but also in south-west England with a few other wild populations, and many inhabit deer parks. Nearly all farmed deer are red deer.

Sika deer, slightly smaller than red deer, were introduced into Scotland in the 1860s. The two species can, and do, interbreed.

Fallow deer have been in Britain since Norman times. They are one of the most important ornamental park species in the UK, with a few herds now living in the wild. One or two farms keep fallow deer.

Roe deer are a small native species that lives in wooded scrubland. Their population is growing rapidly, even encroaching on our towns. They are temperamentally unsuitable for farming but are widely hunted.

Muntjac and Chinese water deer are escapees from deer parks. Not much bigger than large dogs, their population is spreading throughout England and will inevitably reach Scotland. Muntjac can breed all year round.

The cuts of venison and their uses

1. Haunch (back leg): Haunches make splendid bone-in joints. More commonly they are boned into steaks (topside, silverside or pavé), boneless roasts, and diced or sliced for stew and stir-fry. 'Collops' comes from the French 'escalope' and means a thin slice.

2. Saddle (back): Saddle is a bone-in joint. It can be cut into racks or chops, or boned out into loin (roast and

steak) and fillet/tenderloin. These are the most tender pieces.

3. Shoulder: Most commonly sliced or diced for stews and casseroles. It is also boned and rolled for braising. Shoulder cuts from young deer may also be roasted or quick-fried.

4. Neck: Good for mince or making stock. From young deer, diced neck meat makes a good stew.

5. Shank and shin: Usually minced for processing or diced for a slow-cook stew. Can also be trimmed into whole shanks or sliced into osso buco.

6. Flank and brisket: From young deer, these parts can be stuffed and rolled. From older deer, it can be fatty and is either discarded or trimmed for processing.

Recipe finder for each cut

As well as the specific recipes listed here, all these cuts can be made into really good dishes simply by using the general cooking directions at the beginning of each section, along with the suggestions for sauces and vegetables.

Very often, cuts other than the one specified in a recipe can be used so I have indicated them here. Anything marked ★ indicates that the cooking time in the recipe will need adjusting, either because the joint is thicker (see general instructions) or because the cut is tougher and will need longer to cook.

Note: 'medallions' are small, nicely trimmed, round steaks that usually come from the loin or the haunch.

Cut	Recipes
Haunch bone-in joint, shoulder bone-in or rolled joint	29, 30 or use general instructions
Haunch boneless joint	24, 25, 28, 29, 30
Haunch steak, chops, loin steak, pavé, medallions	1–12 or use general instructions
Diced haunch, stir-fry	1–7,★ 9,★ 11,★ 32–35 See p.19 for frying
Saddle joint	Use general instructions
Rack of venison	24, 26, 28; cook as loin
Loin	24, 25, 26, 27,★ 28, 29, 30
Fillet (undercut/tenderloin)	1–12,★ 25,★ 26,★ 27, 28★ or use general instructions
Shoulder steak	32–35, plus 1–7★ and 9–12★ if it's young venison, de-sinewed and served pink
Diced shoulder	32–35
Mince	17–23
Shin, shank and osso buco	29,★ 30,★ 31, 32–35★

Do I really have to . . . marinate?

Many people still worry that it's necessary to spend hours or days marinating venison with expensive ingredients before cooking it. But, just like other meat, it is perfectly all right to cook venison without a marinade. Indeed, good quality venison has such a lovely flavour that it is a shame to disguise it – I much prefer the contrast between pure venison and a complex sauce. Also, the trend for lighter, healthy dishes means that very rich ones are not always appropriate, luscious though they are sometimes. However, there are occasions when it is fun to play around with flavours, especially for those with a lot of venison to eat.

The easiest way to get a 'marinated' flavour is simply to cook the venison slowly in red wine and spices, adding a splash of wine vinegar for a stronger effect. Soaking it in a marinade makes it even stronger. For steaks, an hour is plenty time and for stews and roasts, two or three hours or overnight at most. See pp.84–5 for suggested flavours.

Tip:
If it is an awkward shape, put the joint and marinade into a thick polythene bag and draw the liquid up around the meat. Pat it dry before browning it.

Spice rubs will add interest if needed. See pp.84–5 for complementary spice flavours.

MARINADE · DAY 2

Do I really have to . . . bard and lard?

Barding means wrapping meat in a layer of fat to prevent the outside from drying out. But unless it is a really large roasting joint, then barding is not necessary. Buttered grease-proof paper tied over it and/or basting occasionally will serve nearly as well, and small joints need nothing.

Larding is inserting fat into the meat to keep the centre moist. But if you serve the venison pink there is absolutely no point in larding it, as the juices keep it moist anyway. However, if a joint is to be cooked to well-done, then larding does prevent it becoming dry. Directions are on p.70.

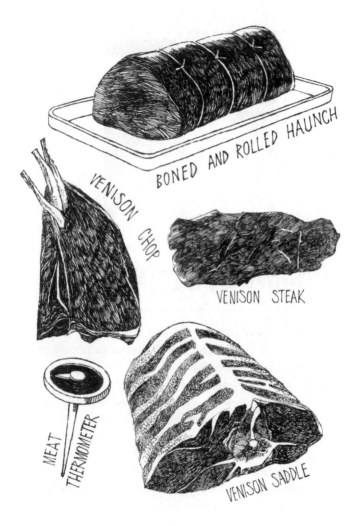

BONED AND ROLLED HAUNCH

VENISON CHOP

VENISON STEAK

MEAT THERMOMETER

VENISON SADDLE

Steaks, stir-fry and chops

PARSLEY

STEAK

Nichola Fletcher's pocket guide to cooking venison steak

Use the right cut: trimmed loin is the most reliably tender cut, no matter what age the deer. From young deer, haunch steaks are beautifully tender, and even shoulder steaks can be fried if left pink. From older deer, haunch steaks can be used but they sometimes turn from pink to dry very quickly, so be warned. Chops are just loin steaks with a little bone attached, so they cook just like steaks and can be substituted for most of the steak recipes.

Fry, grill or oven? because domestic grills are not usually hot enough I don't recommend grilling unless steaks are very thick, because they will overcook before the outside has browned. Frying is much more controllable. Oven temperatures vary, so baking steaks pink is much more difficult to get right, but if covered in a liquid or sauce, baking is a good method for well-done steaks.

On the barbecue: if there is no place to rest steaks when browned, turn them frequently over the coolest part of the fire and serve immediately when done. Alternatively, wrap them in thick foil and leave on the side of the grill to rest and keep warm. A meat thermo-meter helps here.

Thought to remember: it is impossible for pink meat to be dry. It needs no fat to keep it moist.

Another thought: undercooking venison and then allowing it to rest relaxes the steak and also distributes the juices evenly through the meat.

Best for frying: a mixture of butter and oil. Make sure the butter is turning brown before adding steaks.

Cooking time: depends on thickness, not weight – see below. Reduce times if meat is at room temperature, not in the fridge.

Allow steaks to brown: don't push them about. Let them sit still until the pan regains its heat before moving them, otherwise they may throw off water and won't brown.

General technique: 1. Brown steaks in a hot frying pan; 2. Part-cook them by frying at a reduced heat; 3. Rest steaks to relax them and finish the cooking – they only need to keep warm now, not to cook further.

Rare: brown 1 minute per side; fry slowly for 1 minute per cm (½ inch); rest 1 minute per cm.

Medium: brown 1½ minutes per side; fry slowly 1½ minutes per cm (½ inch); rest 1 minute per cm.

Well-done: not recommended but if absolutely necessary, use loin steak, cook as medium, and rest for much longer.

Stir-frying: when frying small chunks or strips of venison, use a very hot pan and serve them immediately they are browned all over – they are too small to need further cooking or resting.

1. Venison steaks with emergency red wine sauce

A more deluxe red wine sauce is on p.89. However, if no stock is available, try this after frying steaks.

Serves 2

2 × 180g (6oz) venison steaks
120ml (4 fl. oz) red wine
10 juniper berries, well crushed
1 tablesp rowan or redcurrant jelly
Soy sauce (optional)

Cook the steaks to taste (see p.19) and remove from the pan to rest in a warm place. Drain off surplus fat but don't allow any of the precious juices to escape. Add red wine and crushed juniper berries to the pan. Stir over a low flame to dissolve the brownings, and to allow the juniper berries to infuse. Then remove the juniper, dissolve the jelly and taste. If it lacks meatiness, add a drop or two of soy sauce, though this is quite salty. Season to taste. Add any juices that come from the resting steaks to the sauce before serving.

VENISON STEAK

2. Venison steaks with red wine and marmalade sauce

Serves 2

This is less strange than it sounds, given that wild duck (another dark, lean meat) is traditionally served with bitter orange sauce. Follow the previous recipe, but substitute bitter marmalade for the jelly. Remove or chop up the peel before serving and adjust the seasoning. The sauce will be hugely better if you can add a tablespoon of reduced stock per person (p.88).

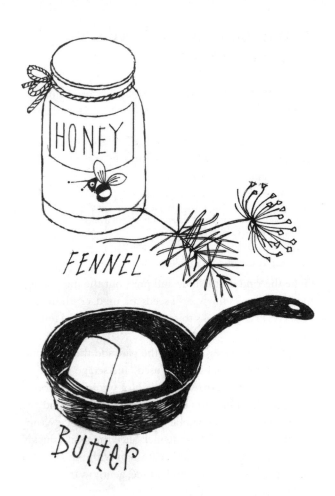

HONEY

FENNEL

Butter

3. Venison steaks with lime, fennel and honey

A quick dish with refreshing summer flavours. Fennel is traditionally served with fish, but actually goes really well with venison.

Serves 2

2 × 180g (6oz) venison steaks
Butter and oil for frying
Juice and rind of a lime
Small handful of fresh fennel leaves (if fresh not available, use 1 teasp fennel seed)
2 teasp honey

Grate the rind off the lime and press out the juice. Chop the fennel leaves finely, or if seeds are used, crush them. Reserve. Fry the steaks to taste (see p.18–19) and remove to rest.

Drain any excess fat from the pan, add the lime rind and juice, and fennel seeds (if used) and scrape up the brown bits in the pan. Add a splash of water if it is too dry, then add honey to taste and season with salt and pepper. Let the sauce bubble gently till it is a nice syrupy texture, then add the fresh fennel. Slice the steaks thickly, return them to the pan and coat them with the sauce. At this stage, if they are too underdone, gently warm them in the sauce to finish them off. Serve at once.

4. Venison steaks with watermelon

This is so simple, but the flavours and textures just work perfectly. You can substitute the seeds of a large pomegranate for the watermelon – it is just as good. It makes a nice starter.

Serves 4

4 × 150g (5oz) venison steaks, medium thick
About ¼ of a watermelon
200g (7oz) watercress
200g (7oz) wild garlic leaves, or rocket
Balsamic syrup

Cut the watermelon into slices about 8mm (¼ inch) thick. Remove the rind and seeds, then slice into strips or small diamond shapes. Wash the watercress thoroughly and spin or pat dry. Remove any tough or discoloured parts and break it into easy-to-eat pieces. Wash and break the rocket similarly and mix them together.

Cook the venison steaks as desired (see p.18–19). While they rest, toss the salad leaves and watermelon together with a good dribble of balsamic syrup and divide it between four plates or bowls. When the steaks are ready, slice them thinly and serve them over, or tossed into, the salad.

5. Fat-free venison steaks with balsamic syrup and raspberries

This recipe was made up at the Royal Highland Show on the spur of the moment by chef Jacqueline O'Donnell from The Sisters restaurant in Glasgow. She wanted to demonstrate a fat-free option using Scottish produce. Everyone liked it so much that I asked if I could write up the recipe for her and share it. Make sure the balsamic is a good quality syrup for best flavour. If your steaks are a different thickness, see p.19 for cooking times.

Serves 2
2 venison steaks (loin, topside or silverside) 1.5cm thick
120g (4oz) fresh raspberries or blackberries
2 teasp balsamic syrup
Sprig of mint to serve

Heat a non-stick frying pan over the stove for 2 minutes with no fat or oil in it. Pat the steaks dry and place them in the hot pan. Cook for 2 minutes each side, till nicely browned. Swirl the balsamic syrup round in the pan, and draw off the heat. Add the raspberries, shake the pan to distribute the balsamic and leave them to warm through for a few minutes while the steaks rest in the pan.

Just before serving, swirl the warmed raspberries

round in the pan once more, then serve them around the steaks on warm plates. Drizzle with the balsamic sauce and decorate with a sprig of mint, if wished.

RASPBERRIES

BALSAMIC SYRUP

MINT

VENISON STEAK

6. Venison chops (or steaks) with aligot

Aligot is a heavenly mash from the Massif Central of France. With cheese, butter, cream and potatoes, it is the complete opposite of the previous recipe but complements venison really well. It makes a brilliant dish for a cold winter's night. Try it with baked venison sausages, too. The chops (or steaks) should be nice and thick, so if they are roe chops cut them in pairs or they will be too thin and dry up. Tomatoes cut in half, drizzled with oil and sprinkled with salt and thyme, then grilled or baked, go very well with this.

Serves 6
6 thick or 12 double chops or steaks

Aligot
800g (1¾lb) potatoes
80g (3oz) butter
1 large garlic clove, crushed
1 heaped tablesp crème fraîche
450g (1lb) tomme d'Auvergne or good-quality sharp cheddar, cut into cubes

---

Boil the potatoes in salted water until tender, then drain and mash them. Then, over a very low heat, beat in the cream, butter and garlic. Gradually add the cheese a handful at a time, beating it in with a wooden spoon.

Once all of the cheese has been incorporated, season
with pepper; it may not need salt. It should have an
elastic texture from beating in all the cheese. Reserve and
keep warm.

Now cook the chops to taste and serve with the
aligot and some grilled tomatoes.

7. Venison stir-fry steak with Stroganoff sauce

The mushrooms in Stroganoff sauce go particularly well with venison, and sour cream gives a nice sharp twist. You don't have to cut the steak into strips, of course; you could cook them whole, in which case use the brandy from the sauce to flame the steaks just before they rest. This goes well with plain rice that has lots of diced, cooked vegetables stirred into it.

Serves 4
650g (1½lb) venison steak
Butter and oil to cook

Sauce
1 large onion, finely chopped
3 cloves garlic, finely chopped
350g (12oz) mushrooms, sliced
2 teasp smoked paprika
2 teasp tomato purée
2 tablesp brandy
300ml (½ pint) venison or beef stock
4 tablesp soured cream (*smetana*)
2 gherkins, finely chopped
Handful of chopped parsley

Make the sauce first, and have any rice cooked and keeping warm. Gently fry the onion and garlic in butter till soft and light brown, then stir in the mushrooms.

Raise the heat a little and cook until the water has evaporated from the mushrooms. Sprinkle on the paprika and stir in the tomato purée. Add the brandy and allow it to cook for a minute or two, then add the stock and boil gently until it is quite thick. Then stir in the sour cream and gherkins and adjust the seasoning. Keep it warm while the venison is cooking and stir in the parsley just before serving.

Slice the venison into chunky, finger-sized strips. Heat a large frying pan with butter and oil and when brown add the strips, making sure they are not crowded – they must brown very quickly or they will start to give off liquid. As soon as one side is browned, turn them and brown the other side. Then simply shake the pan briefly to roll the strips around so that all sides are very briefly cooked. That's all they need – no resting – just serve them immediately with the sauce.

GARLIC

ONION

PARSLEY

31

8. Oven-baked venison steaks

Over the years I have been talking to people about
venison, a great many have said that this is how they like to
cook their venison steak. It is a pretty foolproof recipe –
good for less confident cooks – and ideal for those who
enjoy a thoroughly cooked steak rather than the juicier,
pinker version that many (including me!) prefer.
Everything hinges on the quality of the soup used; some
people use a ready-made sauce instead of the soup.

Serves 4

4 large venison haunch steaks
50g (2oz) butter, chopped into small pieces
1 tin of good-quality cream of mushroom (or celery) soup
    (or use your own home-made soup)
120ml (¼ pint) milk
Freshly ground black pepper

Preheat the oven to 180°C (350°F, Gas 4). Put the
venison steaks into an ovenproof dish and dot the butter
on top of them. Mix together the remaining ingredients
and pour over the steaks. Cover the dish with foil and
bake in the oven for 45 minutes to 1 hour, or until
tender. Taste, and only add salt if necessary – most ready-
made soups will be salty enough. It will happily keep
warm for another 30 minutes, if necessary. Great with
mashed potatoes, and even better if you cook some
celeriac, parsnip or turnip (swede) in with the potatoes.

Venison treasure chest

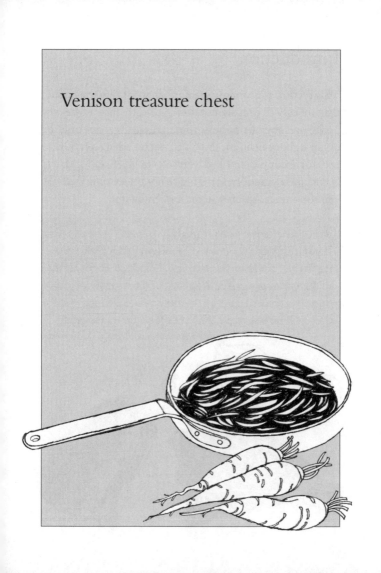

Introduction

This section is a venison treasure chest of different dishes that are easy to prepare but don't fit neatly into a category. Some are obvious starters, some are salads that could be either light or main meals, some contain advice on how to use, for example, smoked venison, or liver and kidneys. Some are suggestions for using that wonderful ingredient, venison mince. So browse on, and enjoy it.

Tip *(applies to the first 3 recipes)*
If you think the meat is too bloody when it is sliced up, return the slices to the frying pan and stir them about in the warm pan juices. Warm them through very gently until well coated, and by the time you are eating them, they will be less rare. Don't overcook them, though.

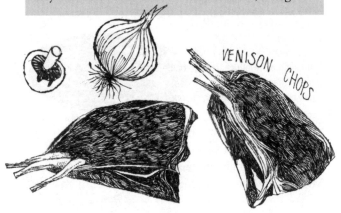

VENISON CHOPS

9. Thai venison salad

Very often when serving a buffet the salad leaves get left to the end, but not these ones – I am often asked for the recipe.

Starter for 4 or main for 2
300g (10oz) thick-cut venison steak (haunch, fillet or loin)

Dressing
2 chillies, finely chopped
2 tablesp Thai fish sauce
2 tablesp runny honey or soft brown sugar
1 tablesp vegetable oil
1 clove garlic, crushed
Juice of 2 limes (roll the limes first to release the juice)
1 tablesp chopped mint leaves

Salad
2 spring onions
1 red onion
½ cucumber
1 small crunchy lettuce (e.g. Romaine)
Handful mangetout peas
Small bunch fresh coriander, chopped

Season the venison with pepper. Cook to rare (see p.19), then draw it off the heat to rest and cool slightly.

Chop the chilli into pieces the size of a match head. Mix these together with the rest of the sauce ingredients, whisking thoroughly to dissolve the honey (warm it if necessary).

Prepare the salad so that everything is sliced to an even size: separate the red onion slices into segments. Cut the cucumber into matchsticks. Chop the coriander coarsely. Put it all in a bowl, pour over half of the dressing and mix it all together.

Divide the salad between plates or arrange onto a large platter. Slice the meat very thinly and arrange on top. Drizzle with the remaining dressing.

CORIANDER

Honey

10. Sliced venison steak with vegetable ribbons

It's much easier to demonstrate this simple recipe than to describe it in words. You need a large frying pan for the vegetables, and cooking tongs are ideal to gently lift and turn them as they cook. Use the leftover cores of the carrot and courgettes for soup, stews or stock. See p.19 for how to cook the venison.

Serves 4

600–800g (1¼–1¾lb) venison steak, thick cut
85g (3oz) smoked streaky bacon, snipped into pieces
2 large, thick carrots, peeled
2 slim leeks
2 courgettes
1 clove of garlic, crushed
1 tablesp finely chopped or sliced fresh ginger
Zest of ½ a lemon or lime
Juice of 1 lemon or lime
Handful of chopped parsley or coriander

Gently fry the bacon until golden brown. Reserve and keep warm.

Cut the leeks into 15cm (6in.) lengths. Discard any coarse outer and top leaves from the leeks, cut off the root, and slice the rest in four lengthways to produce fine strips rather than rings. Wash thoroughly to remove any grit, and pat dry. Using a potato peeler, slice off thin ribbons of carrot lengthways. Turn the carrot round as you slice, and continue for as long as you can make strips. Repeat this procedure with the courgette.

Sweat the leeks, garlic and ginger in oil over a low flame, turning them gently with tongs until they start to soften. Add the carrot and continue the cooking gently, again turning them carefully with tongs until the carrot becomes floppy, then add the courgette and lime zest. Cook and turn for a further minute or so, until the courgette starts to become translucent. Be careful not to overcook, or the ribbons will break up. Stir in the lemon or lime juice and keep it warm.

Cook the venison to rare/medium – see p.19. To serve, place the vegetables with their juices in a large warm dish or onto individual plates. Slice the steak thinly and pile the slices on top of the vegetables. Sprinkle the bacon pieces on top, along with the parsley/coriander.

CARROT   STREAKY BACON

11. Warm venison salad with pickled blackberries

This is just a suggestion; you can alter this any way you like depending on the salad ingredients available. You could try it on top of thinly sliced roasted root vegetables in the wintertime.

Starter for 4 or light main for 2
300g (10oz) venison haunch, fillet or loin steak
4 portions (2 small bags) mixed herbs and baby salad leaves
3 tablesp olive or walnut oil
1 capful cider vinegar or white wine vinegar
Black pepper and sea salt flakes to season
Pickled blackberries (see p.90) or caperberries

Put the salad leaves and herbs in a bowl. Strew some flaked sea salt over them and grind in some black pepper. Add the oil and vinegar and mix the salad well. Divide between the plates or large shallow bowls. Cook the venison to taste (see p.19). Slice it thinly and pile it over the salad. Pour any pan juices over the meat after placing it on the salad, and dot with the pickled blackberries/caperberries, if used.

12. The best-ever venison sandwich

September 4th is national Eat Scottish Venison Day. At its launch in 2009, Tom Lewis of Monachyle Mhor cooked this on the lawn in front of Blair Castle. It made one of the best breakfasts I've ever had. The secret with barbecuing venison is to have a place to the side of the fire where you can rest thick pieces of meat (steaks or small roasts) covered in foil to keep them warm. Thinly sliced meat is much easier to eat in a sandwich than a whole steak. The bread for this should be so delicious that you could eat it on its own.

Serves 4
650g (1½lb) venison loin or slim pieces of haunch
4 small or 2 large baguettes
200g (7oz) fresh chanterelles or other mushrooms
2 cloves garlic, finely chopped
Thyme or other herbs, to taste

On a tray or in a pan, cook the chanterelles in butter with the garlic and thyme till soft but not disintegrating. Season and set aside to keep warm. Brush the venison with oil and, once the barbecue has subsided to a hot grey ash, start to cook it. Allow all surfaces to brown quickly and then turn it frequently to cook the meat evenly. Use a meat thermometer to find out when it is cooked. Toast the outside of the baguettes on the barbecue. Split lengthways and butter them.

Place a quarter of the chanterelles on each of the four halves of bread, slice the venison thinly and lay it on top, then cover with the rest of the bread. Make sure everyone is ready and waiting to eat it.

VENISON

GARLIC

MEAT THERMOMETER

THYME

13. Four serving suggestions for smoked venison

Smoked venison is endlessly versatile. Here are some suggestions to get you going. Try it:

i. with pickled cucumber (soak thin slices of cucumber in the Thai dressing on p.35). Serve it with the picked blackberries or damsons on p.90.

ii. made into little patties with citrus sauce. Chop a small onion finely. Chop 175g (6oz) smoked venison finely too. Mix together and season with black pepper, then press into four round pastry cutters. Set aside some thin strips of orange zest for garnish, then squeeze the juice of 1 orange and 2 lemons into a jug. Whisk in 2 tablespoons of good quality oil and moisten the venison patties. Lift off the cutters and serve, garnished with orange zest.

iii. with good horseradish sauce and cooked beetroot cut into matchsticks.

iv. with fried pineapple. Slice some peeled and cored pineapple thinly and fry these in hot butter over a high heat till golden brown on each side. Slice into strips and sprinkle them with medium-hot paprika. Then drizzle some balsamic syrup over them and serve with the smoked venison.

14. Potted hough

I tried spicing this up but actually it is by far the best in
its simplest form. Either spread it on bread or serve with
pickled caperberries or gherkins. You can also stir it into a
meat-based risotto or serve it with salad. The sinew on
the knuckles makes the jelly set. There is usually some
flavoursome but pale stock left over.

Makes lots
2 venison shanks, including the knuckle with sinew
1 extra knuckle with sinew
Salt and pepper

Pack the shanks and knuckles tightly into a large pot and
cover amply with water. Cover and bring to the boil.
Reduce heat and simmer gently for 4–5 hours until the
meat falls off the bone. Take meat
off the bone, discarding all sinews,
bone, etc. Strain the stock into a clean
pan. Slice the meat finely across the
grain using a very sharp knife and
place in a clean pan. Cover
generously with strained stock and
season it well. Ladle into moulds
and put in the fridge to cool and
set. You can freeze this successfully
for 2–3 months.

15. Venison liver, kidneys and heart

Venison offal is similar in many ways to lamb's so you can use any lamb recipes successfully. However, although roe offal is about the same size as lamb's, red deer offal is about three times larger. It is so delicious that I think it is best cooked very simply. Just one word of warning: when the males – especially red and sika – are rutting (July–September for roe, September–November for fallow, red and sika, and November–January for Chinese water deer), and for a while afterwards, liver and kidneys can become extremely strong and are enough to put anyone off offal for life.

Liver

Venison liver in particular is a real treat and just needs slicing thinly and frying very quickly. As with all fried liver, don't overcook it or it toughens and tastes bitter. Serve it with lemon juice and parsley, or fried snippets of bacon, or a brandy cream sauce with some extra good mash with thyme and maybe crushed juniper berries stirred into it. Alternatively, it can be very gently braised in liquid till cooked through – don't hurry this or it will overcook.

Kidneys

Kidneys may be cut in half and grilled, chopped and fried, or added to a stew. Classic combinations are garlic, mushrooms and cream, or mustard mash if you like a hot kick with them.

Heart

The heart is a muscle, not an organ, so its meat is like very fine-grained steak. It's one of my favourites. Like liver, to make sure it stays tender, heart needs to be sliced and fried quickly, or else very slowly stewed. If fried, it can be used for many of the steak recipes.

THYME

16. Archie Crawford's venison pâté

Archie Crawford was one of the earliest deer farmers in the UK; he developed this pâté at his farm near Beauly, in Inverness-shire.

900g (2lb) venison liver
2 medium onions
Butter and oil for frying
2 medium cloves garlic
225g (½lb) smoked streaky bacon
225g (½lb) butter
150ml (¼ pint) double cream
Salt, pepper, thyme, parsley
¼ wine glass brandy

Chop the onions finely and fry them slowly in butter and oil. Chop the bacon finely and fry that too. Chop the liver into small chunks, discarding any tubes. Chop the garlic finely. Now mix all the ingredients (except for the brandy) together, cover with foil, and bake at 180°C (350°F, Gas 4) for 45 minutes. Remove from the oven, add the brandy and stir it around. Then blend to a smooth consistency, put it into pots and chill.

17. The best mince in the world

Venison mince is one of the tastiest of all and has an honorable history: not many people know that the original recipe for chilli con carne uses venison, not beef. It is fantastic used in all pasta dishes, or as simple mince 'n' tatties, or brilliant topped with sliced tomatoes and a browned cheese sauce.

For full-flavoured mince, thorough browning and lengthy cooking is the secret. Brown your onions first in a large frying pan, then remove. Add a bit more fat or oil and the venison mince. Because it is so lean, it forms a solid mass in the frying pan. Turn the heat up high, and use a fish slice to start breaking it up into crumbs. This will take some time, as a lot of water gets thrown off, but keep at it and eventually it will start to brown. It needs to be deep brown all over. Then stir in about a tablespoon of flour to each 500g (1lb 2oz) of mince, then add the onions and your liquid (water, stock, wine, etc.). Cover

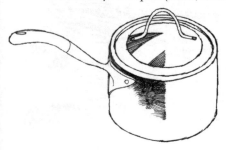 the pan and allow it to simmer for about an hour until it is really tender. It will need stirring from time to time, and topping up with water. Season, and enjoy.

18. Meatballs, burgers, sausagemeat and pies

The basic mixture for all of these is similar, though flavour combinations are endless – see pp.84–5 for more suggestions. Because venison is lean and will be cooked through, it is necessary to improve the succulence to prevent it feeling dry. Here are some tips and a few recipes.

Add succulence: This usually comes from fat, and you can add fat such as belly pork, bacon, or lamb or beef fat. If you prefer not to add fat, add cooked vegetables such as onions, mushrooms, sweet peppers, aubergine, soaked prunes or apricots. Tempting though it may be, I wouldn't use venison fat, as it has a high melting point and sticks to your mouth when eating it.

Add flavour: Any spice that you enjoy can of course be used and there are many good ready-made spice mixes available. Here are some of my favourites. *Spices*: juniper berries, dried ginger, nutmeg. *Herbs*: parsley, lovage, coriander, thyme, mint, fennel, garlic, fresh ginger.

Meatballs: Make them really small so that there is a lot of outside to get coated in the sauce, and make sure the sauce has a succulent texture. Fresh tomato sauce always goes well.

Burgers: Although food hygiene advice is always to cook minced meat products all the way through to 75°C (165°F), many rebels prefer to take the risk and cook them pink, since venison is inherently a healthy meat. If cooked pink it is less necessary to add in vegetables or fat to keep them moist. Some people like to add an egg to bind the mixture together.

Sausagemeat: Traditionally these have the most added fat (20–30 per cent) and are cooked in skins. However, if making sausagemeat for sausage rolls, terrines or raised pies, the fat content can be reduced to 15–20 per cent. A binder such as oatmeal or breadcrumbs is traditional with British sausages – add about 85g (3oz) per 500g (1lb 2oz) mince.

Basic proportions
500g (1lb 2oz) lean venison mince
175g (6oz) fat or succulence (as above)
Salt and pepper
2 teasp spices, mixed (as above)
2 tablesp chopped fresh herbs (as above)

---

19. Venison meatballs with North African spices

Serves 4

Basic mix as p. 50. For succulence use 50g (2oz) soaked prunes, 50g (2oz) apricots and 75g (2 tablespoons) peppers and onion sautéed in oil. For the spices, use 1 tablespoon of tagine spices. Chop everything really finely, as it makes the meatballs easier to form. Mix everything together and make little meatballs about 2cm (1in.) in diameter. Fry, and serve with couscous.

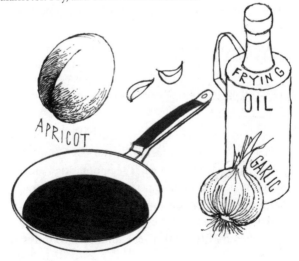

20. Venison meatballs with aubergine and mint

Serves 4

Basic mix as p. 50. For succulence, use 1 large aubergine, 1 medium onion and 50g (2oz) bacon. For flavour use 2 tablespoons chopped fresh mint, 1 teaspoon ground turmeric, 1 teaspoon grated fresh ginger. Slice the aubergine lengthways and bake in a microwave on full power for 5 minutes or until tender. When cool enough, scrape out the flesh. Chop everything finely, mix together and make little meatballs about 3cm (1½in.) in diameter.

21. Venison burgers

Makes 6–8 burgers

Basic mix as p. 50. For succulence use 120g (4oz) minced bacon and 50g (2oz) onion. For flavour use 1 clove crushed garlic, pepper and salt, 1 teaspoon dried ginger, 1 teaspoon ground nutmeg, 1 teaspoon crushed juniper berries and 1 tablespoon chopped fresh parsley.

Thoroughly mix all the ingredients and form into patties, then fry, grill or barbecue until cooked through.

22. Gourmet sausage rolls

Makes up to 24

For the filling you can use ready-made sausages or any of the mixtures p. 50. If using sausages, remove the skins, because they go rubbery. Roll out a 500g (1lb 2oz) pack of puff or shortcrust pastry to a 55 × 25cm (22 × 10in.) rectangle. Cut it lengthways to make two long strips. Put half of the sausagemeat lengthways onto each half, moisten the edges of the pastry with water and roll the pastry over the sausagemeat to form two long rolls with the seams underneath. Press to seal the edges. Brush the top with beaten egg and cut into 24 pieces. Place onto baking sheets and cook at 190°C (375°F, Gas 5) for 20–25 minutes until the pastry is golden brown and the sausagemeat cooked through.

23. Venison terrine

Makes approx. 1.2kg (2½lbs)

Use 650g (1½lb) of any of the mixtures in this section so far. You will also need 225g (8oz) venison steak and 250g (9oz) prunes, soaked overnight in brandy and sliced lengthways. Line a greased loaf tin with 350g (12oz) very thin-cut rindless streaky bacon. Pack a layer of sausage-meat tightly in the base. Cut steak into strips and lay strips in the sausagemeat, alternating with prunes. Repeat with layers of sausagemeat, steak strips and prunes till the tin is full. Fold bacon over the top and press firmly down. Wrap tin completely in foil, place in a deep dish and add water to halfway up tin. Cook in a medium oven (180°C, 350°F, Gas 4) for 2 hours. Allow to cool completely before turning out of the tin. Chill thoroughly before slicing with a sharp, hot knife.

STREAKY BACON

PRUNES

Roasting venison

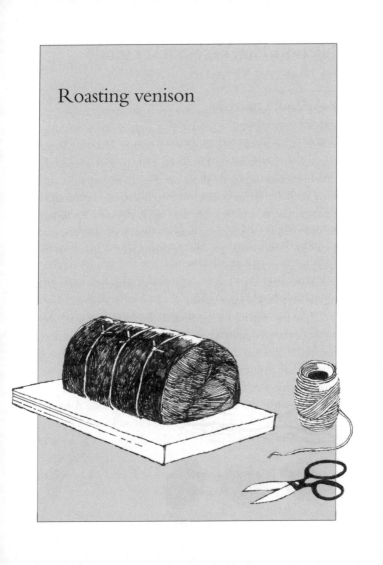

Nichola Fletcher's pocket guide to roasting venison

Once you understand how to roast venison, recipes are rather unnecessary – it is often just a question of deciding which sauce and vegetables to serve with it. There are some suggestions on pp.83–96. However, some recipes use slightly different cooking methods or need extra preparation, so I have included them below. No two ovens run at the same temperature, no matter what they say, so the only absolutely reliable way of making sure your venison is cooked the way you like it is to use a meat thermometer – they can be bought for under £10.

Essential tip: use a meat thermometer – you will never overcook a joint again.

Use the right cut: saddle and loin are the most reliably tender cuts, no matter what age the deer. From young deer, haunch is also beautifully tender. From older deer, haunch can be roasted but it can turn from pink to dry very quickly, so always undercook it.

Thought to remember: it is impossible for pink meat to be dry. Undercooking venison and then allowing it to rest relaxes the meat and also distributes the juices evenly.

Don't like pink meat? braise it instead and cook to well-done. See next chapter.

Cooking times: depend on thickness as much as weight – see below. In all cases brown the joint all over before placing in the oven, and preheat the oven to 230°C (450°F, Gas 8). Ideal resting temperature is 80°C (170°F, Gas ¼). Reduce times if meat is at room temperature, not in the fridge. Bone-in joints need a little longer to cook. Joints with a thick covering of fat also need extra time.

Using a meat thermometer: use timings below as a guide, but for real accuracy stop the high-temperature cooking when it reaches 45°C/115°F for rare(50°C/ 120°F for medium) and then rest until it reads 55–60°C/130–140°F (60–65°C/140–150°F).

MEAT THERMOMETER

Rough guideline for bone-in joints
For rare: roast for 2½ minutes per 1cm (½in.), then rest for 2 minutes per 1cm (½in.).

For medium: roast for 3 minutes per 1cm (½in.), then rest for 3 minutes per 1cm (½in.).

Rough guideline for boneless joints
For rare: roast for 2 minutes per 1cm (½in.), then rest for 2–3 minutes per 1cm (½in.).

For medium: roast for 3 minutes per 1cm (½in.), then rest for 2–3 minutes per 1cm (½in.).

On the barbecue: after cooking, wrap the joint in thick foil and leave on a plate at the side of the grill to rest and keep warm.

24. Venison saddle with beetroot

This is based around Escoffier's classic recipe for saddle of hare. Hare and venison have a lot in common, both being dark, rich meats. The slightly acidulated beetroot is a similar flavour pairing to red cabbage.

Serves 4

750g (1lb 10oz) venison loin
180g (6oz) streaky dry-cured bacon cut into small strips
Salt and black pepper
300ml (½ pint) double cream
1 heaped teasp plain flour
300ml (½ pint) boiling water
675g (1½lb) cooked beetroot, chopped finely
100g (3oz) butter
1 tablesp red wine vinegar

Preheat the oven to 190°C (375°F, Gas 5). With a sharp knife make incisions in the meat and insert half of the bacon into the holes. In a fireproof casserole, gently heat the remaining bacon until the fat seeps out, add the venison, and gently brown it all over in the fat. Then season it with salt and pepper, pour over half of the cream, and put it in the oven for 15 minutes, basting the meat twice. The cream may separate at this stage. Then remove the meat and keep it warm.

Stir the flour into the casserole until smooth, then stir in the boiling water. Once smooth, stir in the rest of the cream and bring it to the boil. Adjust the seasoning, and keep warm.

Re-heat the cooked beetroot with the butter, add the vinegar, and season with salt and pepper if necessary.

Slice the venison onto a serving dish and arrange the beetroot around the meat. Spoon a small amount of sauce over the sliced meat to stop it drying out and serve the rest in a sauceboat.

25. Venison Wellington

This is endlessly popular, delicious and filling. You can line the pastry with pâté instead of mushrooms, which makes it even richer. It's important that the meat is the right shape. Make sure it is an even, cylindrical piece about 5–6cm in diameter. If you use roe deer loin, tie two together or it may be too thin and overcook. If your piece is thicker, use a meat thermometer to make sure it is cooked correctly.

Serves 4
900g (2lb) venison loin or boneless haunch
80g (3oz) butter
2 cloves garlic, finely chopped
350g (12oz) mushrooms/fungi, finely chopped
Salt, black pepper
2 tablesp fresh chopped parsley
1 tablesp fresh thyme leaves
450g (1lb) pure butter puff pastry
Beaten egg to glaze

Brown the meat all over in butter and oil in a frying pan, keeping it nice and flat. Then reduce the heat in the frying pan and keep turning the meat for a further 5 minutes. Remove and allow it to cool completely (45–60 minutes).

For the mushroom filling, heat the butter in the unwashed frying pan. Add the garlic, and the minute it starts to brown, add the mushrooms. Allow these to cook and reduce until they look buttery rather than watery. Season with salt and pepper, stir in the parsley and thyme and let this cool as well.

When ready to cook it, preheat the oven to 220°C (425°F, Gas 7). Roll out the pastry in a rectangle big enough to wrap your joint with an overlap of 3cm (1½in.) all round. Brush the overlap with beaten egg. Spread the mushroom mixture inside this, place the meat on top and wrap it in the pastry. Turn the meat so that the sealed edge is underneath. Seal the ends thoroughly, remove excess pastry, and press firmly all over to make sure it is well sealed.

Decorate the top if wished, and glaze with the remaining egg. Insert the meat thermometer in one end and bake in the oven for 15 minutes, or until the pastry is golden and puffed. Then reduce the heat to 160°C (325°F, Gas 3) and cook for another 10–15 minutes, depending on the degree of rare-medium desired. Your meat thermometer will tell you when it is perfect.

26. Loin of venison with claret sauce

Many years ago, I shared a game-cooking demonstration with chef John Woods at a Food and Film Fiesta in London. We hadn't met beforehand but between us we cooked up eight game recipes in less than an hour; this is one of his. The cooking times are based on the meat being 6–7cm (about 1½in.) thick. See p.57 if it is different. As with so many sauces, this calls for strong stock (see p.88), which gives that lovely rich, silky finish. John served this with red cabbage and rösti potatoes.

Serves 4
675g (1½lb) venison loin
3 shallots, chopped
2 wineglasses claret or other red wine
4 juniper berries, crushed
450ml (¾ pint) strong venison or game stock
150g (5oz) carrots and onions, chopped
100g (4oz) button mushrooms, chopped
Small handful of chives, chopped
2 large fresh tomatoes, peeled and diced

To make the sauce, chop the shallots and brown them in a pan, add claret and juniper berries and simmer for 10 minutes. Add the strong stock and allow it to reduce gently. Sear and brown the venison in a hot pan and remove. Add the carrots and shallots to the same pan and brown them too. Put the venison back on top of the vegetables, add a ladleful of the claret sauce, and put the pan into a hot oven 220°C (450°F, Gas 8) for 8–10 minutes. Remove from the pan and rest it for 5–10 minutes.

Pour the reduced sauce into the roasting pan and stir to amalgamate the flavours, then strain off the sauce, pressing all the precious juices out. Add the button mushrooms and simmer briskly till they are cooked and the sauce has reduced to a syrup. Just before serving add the diced tomato and chives and warm through. Slice the venison and divide it between four plates with the sauce.

27. Super-fast venison fillet with Parma ham, courgettes and butter bean mash

A year or two ago I was asked to judge a venison cookery competition at the Game Conservancy Scottish Fair at Scone. The winner was Ally Bremner from Melrose, who is better known as a world-class fly fisher. As well as the venison being perfectly cooked, I liked the contrast of the earthy butter bean mash with the salty Parma ham and the barely cooked buttery courgette. You need a tender, log-shaped piece of meat here, 5cm (2in.) in diameter.

Serves 4

750g (1lb 10oz) venison loin or fillet
1 tablesp chopped fresh herbs, e.g. parsley, thyme, marjoram
6 juniper berries
2 tablesp redcurrant jelly
4 slices of Parma ham
2 tablesp red wine

400g (14oz) can of butter beans, drained
2 tablesp crème fraîche
2 courgettes
2 teasp unsalted butter
Pinch of nutmeg

Preheat the oven to 225°C (450°F, Gas 8). Chop the fresh herbs (you'll need about a tablespoon once chopped) and the juniper berries finely and stir them into the redcurrant jelly. Spread this over the venison and wrap it with the Parma ham, making sure all the ends are underneath the meat so it doesn't unravel. Roast in the oven for 10–15 minutes, according to taste. Allow to rest in a warm place.

Meanwhile lightly crush the butter beans with the crème fraîche in a small pan over a low heat to gently warm them, adding salt and pepper to taste. Grate the courgettes on a large grating disc, and just before serving melt the butter in a shallow pan and stir the courgettes over a medium heat for barely a minute – they will cook very quickly and should still be bright green. Add the nutmeg and serve with the butter bean mash and the sliced venison.

THYME

Crème FRAÎCHE

PARSLEY

28. Spice-rubbed venison with lime risotto

The lime-flavoured risotto sets off these spices nicely but the recipe can be altered greatly by using different ones. If you like a little chilli kick, then add ¼–½ teaspoon. As with any risotto, the vegetables should be changed according to the season. You could also serve this with Asian noodles that are cooked in stock with a tablespoon of Thai fish sauce, and plenty of chopped fresh herbs (mint, coriander, etc.) stirred into them.

ONION

NUTMEG

BONED AND ROLLED HAUNCH

The risotto takes 30–40 minutes, so start cooking the venison after about 10–15 minutes so everything is ready at the same time.

Serves 4–6
900g (2lb) venison loin or rolled haunch
3 cardamom pods
½ teasp green peppercorns
½ teasp grated nutmeg
1 teasp coriander seeds
2 whole star anise or ½ teasp powdered

Lime risotto
2 unwaxed limes, juice and grated zest
4 shallots or 2 small onions, chopped
4 tablesp olive or grapeseed oil
350g (12oz) risotto rice
200ml (⅓ pint) dry white wine
1 litre (1½ pints) venison stock
350g (12oz) asparagus spears, cut into 3cm (1in.) pieces
100g (4oz) baby broad beans
100g (4oz) petit pois
80g (3oz) freshly grated Parmesan
Small bunch fresh coriander, chopped

CORIANDER

Brown the venison all over in hot butter and oil, then remove from the pan and allow it to cool slightly. Heat up a pan without oil and toast the spices for 3–4 minutes but don't let them burn. Cool. Grind them in a pestle and mortar and scatter them over a sheet of cling film. Roll the joint in the spices so that it is covered evenly all over. Wrap it tightly in the cling film and leave for at least 2 hours at room temperature. Cook it (see p.57), cutting out the browning stage.

For the risotto, heat the oil in a large, deep frying pan, and gently fry the shallots until transparent. Add the rice and fry gently for 5 minutes, then add the wine and lime juice. Increase the heat and add a quarter of the stock and the tougher ends of the asparagus. Once this stock is absorbed, add another quarter and keep stirring. Repeat, and when the third quarter of stock is added, put in the middle parts of the asparagus and grind some black pepper into the risotto. With the final quarter of stock, add the broad beans, peas, asparagus tips and the lime zest. Add salt to taste. Finally, stir in the Parmesan to give a creamy finish, and scatter the chopped fresh coriander over it before serving with the sliced venison.

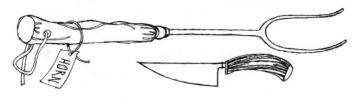

Slow-cooking venison

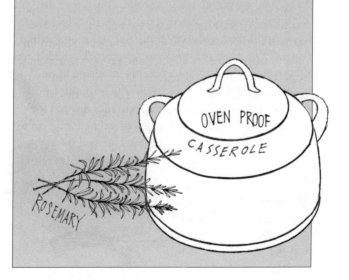

OVEN PROOF

CASSEROLE

ROSEMARY

When and how to lard venison

A good basic casserole is generally cooked by browning
the meat and vegetables, adding spices if wanted, with a
handful of pearl barley if wished, then covering with
liquid and simmering or baking for 2–3 hours. Below are
some suggestions for something a bit different, when you
want a change.

When and how to lard venison

Venison is so lean that cooking it to well-done (i.e. not
pink) means that it can dry out. The easiest way to keep it
moist is to cut up the meat and stew it in a liquid. But if
you want to slow-roast or braise a whole joint, it is best to
lard it. It's easy to do. Just stab the joint with a sharp little
knife to make many small holes, and press some sort of fat
(or solidified oil) deep down into them. Add a little
liquid to the dish when you cook it, and use this to
baste the joint from time to time. Alternatively,
keep the joint completely covered in liquid,
both while it cooks and after it is sliced.

Tip
To make it easier to press
the fat into the holes, cut
it into fingers and pop
it in the freezer to harden.

LARDING

29. Venison haunch braised in red wine

A classic way of slow-cooking a venison joint, but try also using these ingredients with diced venison for a red wine casserole. Haunch is best here, though if it is young or farmed, shoulder is excellent. Either rolled or bone-in joints are good, though rolled gives a neater slice. Serve it with a slightly bitter-sweet vegetable such as spinach or kale, and some glazed carrots.

Serves 6–8

1.5kg (3½lbs) haunch of venison
Butter or lard for larding
2 large onions, sliced
6 sticks of celery, finely chopped
1 teasp ground ginger
1 teasp ground nutmeg
8 juniper berries, crushed
¼ teasp ground cloves
200g (7oz) chopped tinned tomatoes
½ bottle red wine
2 teasp balsamic vinegar
450ml (¾ pint) venison or beef stock (or water)
Butter and flour for *beurre manié* (optional)

Preheat the oven to 200°C (400°F, Gas 6). Lard the meat (see p.70). Then brown it all over in a frying pan and remove to a lidded ovenproof casserole. Brown the onions and add those along with the celery. Mix the spices together, scatter them over the meat and stir them in. Then add the tomatoes, wine, balsamic vinegar and stock (or water). Cover the dish and cook for half an hour, then lower the oven to 180°C (350°F, Gas 4) and cook for a further 1½–2 hours. Turn the joint over from time to time to keep it moist and top up with water or wine if necessary. Young venison and tender cuts may be cooked in the shorter time; old venison will need longer.

Once cooked, slice the meat, making sure the slices are kept submerged in some of the delicious gravy so they can't dry out. Now choose: either serve it in the sauce with the vegetables still in it, or else strain off the sauce and reduce it if necessary. Season to taste. If you prefer a thick sauce, put it in a pan and thicken it with *beurre manié*: mash together equal quantities of butter and flour – about 30g (1oz) butter with a tablespoon of flour – and then whisk this briskly into the sauce until smooth and thick. Don't allow it to boil or it may split.

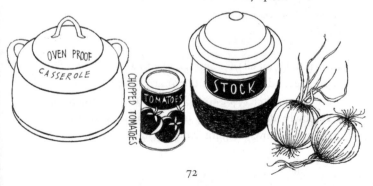

30. Sticky-glazed venison joint

The venison here is covered in liquid so it doesn't need larding. You end up with some useful stock to freeze for future use. Boneless venison is easier to handle, but if you prefer to cook it on the bone, increase the weight by 350g (12oz).

Serves 4
900g (2lbs) boneless haunch or shoulder
350g (12oz) mixed chopped vegetables (onions, root vegetables, celery)

Glaze
1 medium onion, finely chopped
50g (2oz) butter
1 orange, juice and pulp
2 tablesp tomato purée
1 teasp salt
½ teasp ground ginger
½ teasp allspice
2 tablesp Worcestershire sauce
2 tablesp wine vinegar

Brown the joint all over and remove to a pan. Brown the vegetables and add them to the joint. Completely cover it with warm water, bring to the boil gently, and simmer very slowly until tender: 2–3 hours, depending on the cut. Then remove the joint from the stock and allow it to drain.

To make the glaze, gently cook the onions in butter till golden and transparent. Add the remaining ingredients with 150ml (¼ pint) water and simmer until it is like a jam.

When ready to finish the meat, preheat the oven to 230°C (450°F, Gas 8). Lift the joint out of its stock and pat it dry. Put it into an ovenproof dish and coat all surfaces with the glaze. Bake the meat until the coating is dark and sticky – you may need to baste it onto the surface. If the joint was warm when it went into the oven, it will be cooked. If it was cooked from cold, reduce the heat to 160°C (325°F, Gas 3) for a further 20–30 minutes to allow it to cook through.

31. Venison shanks with a hint of chocolate

I love the gelatinous texture of shin and shank. I've used whole shanks here but of course 180g (6oz) per person of diced shin or shoulder will work equally well. Alternatively, use osso buco (sliced shin), allowing 350g (12oz) per person to allow for the bone. Red deer shanks make a normal portion for two; roe shanks give one portion each. Unsweetened cocoa (not drinking chocolate) lends a velvety richness to the sauce. Serve this with extra buttery mash made special by stirring in some mustard or horseradish sauce, or by cooking celeriac or turnip with it.

Serves 2–4

½–1 shank per person (or see above)
350g (12oz) diced vegetables (onions, root vegetables, celery)
10 juniper berries, crushed
1 teasp ground or grated ginger
½ teasp ground nutmeg
1 tablesp cocoa powder
1 teasp tomato purée
120ml (4fl. oz) concentrated venison stock
Juice of 2 oranges
150ml (¼ pint) red wine
1 tablesp brandy
½ teasp balsamic syrup

Preheat the oven to 180°C (350°F, Gas 4). Brown the shanks and remove to a casserole. Brown the vegetables, then remove the pan from the heat. Mix the spices and cocoa powder together evenly, then scatter them over the browned vegetables and stir together. Then stir in the liquids to dissolve the pan brownings. Tip this over the shanks, bring to simmering point, cover and cook in the oven for 3–5 hours until the meat is tender. Adjust the salt and pepper at this point. Remove the shanks carefully (large ones are inclined to fall apart) to serving plates and keep warm. Either serve the vegetables and sauce together with the shanks, or strain the gravy from the vegetables and reduce to a syrupy texture if wished.

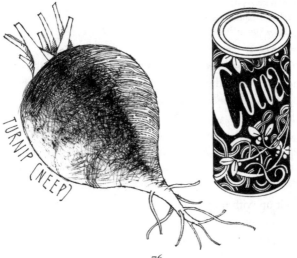

TURNIP (NEEP)

Cocoa

32. Thai-spiced venison casserole

This casserole arose from tipping some left-over dipping sauce into a stew; I was delighted with the result. If you don't have sherry, use 450ml (¾ pint) dry white wine and reduce the water/stock to 150ml (¼ pint). I'd serve this with a generous selection of roasted root vegetables and some fresh green salad or other light vegetable.

Serves 4–6

900g (2lbs) diced venison haunch or shoulder
2 generous tablesp honey
4 teasp Thai green curry sauce
6 tablesp soy sauce
4 teasp miso paste
300ml (½ pint) dry sherry
300ml water or stock

Preheat the oven to 180°C (350°F/Gas 4). Brown the meat all over and place it in an ovenproof casserole. Mix together the honey, curry sauce, soy and miso paste, then add the sherry/white wine gradually until thoroughly combined. Mix this into the meat and add the rest of the liquid as required.

Bring slowly to the boil, then cook for 1½–3 hours, depending on how tender your meat is. You may need to top it up with more water if it gets a bit dry. Taste it at the end but you rarely need to add salt. You can happily make this in advance, as it improves on keeping.

33. Venison casserole with spiced apricots

This is a variation on the previous recipe. I'd serve this with couscous, perhaps with cooked sweet peppers stirred into it. *Ras-el-hanout* is a mixture of at least a dozen different spices – traditionally the spice-seller's best. It doesn't have chilli in it so this is fragrant rather than hot spicing. If you prefer a hot spice, use harissa, which is also a complex mixture but includes chilli. And of course you could do something similar using Indian spices instead – the cooking method is the same. These spice mixes vary in strength so only add half to start with and add more halfway through, only if necessary.

Serves 4–6

900g (2lbs) diced venison haunch or shoulder
2 large onions, peeled and chopped
200g (7oz) dried apricots
1–2 tablesp *ras-el-hanout*
600ml (1 pint) white wine or water

Preheat the oven to 180°C (350°F, Gas 4). Brown the onions and then the meat in batches and put them in an ovenproof casserole. Add the apricots, scatter 1 tablespoon of the spices over the top and stir them in, then add the liquid. Cook as in the previous recipe but check the spices halfway through and add more if needed.

34. Haunch of venison with walnuts and pomegranate

A marvellous rich winter dish from Persia, hence the pomegranate, but a tart rowan jelly tastes incredibly similar. It may sound strange to cook walnuts with meat but they cook down to a wonderful soft texture that goes well with venison.

Serves 6

1kg (2¼lb) boned and rolled venison haunch
125g (4oz) butter or other fat for larding
100ml (3½ fl. oz) pomegranate syrup, or 3 tablesp rowan jelly
150g (5oz) freshly shelled walnuts
1 large onion, finely chopped
600ml (1 pint) venison stock
Salt and pepper
Juice of a lemon (optional)

Lard the meat (see p.70). Brown the meat all over, then put it in an ovenproof dish with a quarter of the stock in the base. Cover with a lid or foil and cook for 2½–3 hours at 180°C (350°F, Gas 4), basting several times.

Chop the walnuts into small crumbs and fry gently in a teaspoon of oil, stirring for about 15 minutes until they darken. Fry the onion in a little oil till golden brown and add to the walnuts along with the rest of the stock. Simmer for 45 minutes. Add the pomegranate juice (or rowan jelly) and pour the sauce over the joint. It is very rich, so serve refreshing vegetables with it.

BONED AND ROLLED HAUNCH

Salt

STOCK

35. Venison stewed with Seville oranges

Seville oranges are only available for a few weeks every January. They are more commonly used for marmalade or to make the classic dish of wild duck with oranges. However, any dark gamey meat benefits from this treatment. If you use normal sweet oranges, make sure they are unwaxed, and reduce or omit the sugar.

Serves 4–6

900g (2lb) diced venison haunch
2 onions
½ teasp cinnamon
½ teasp turmeric
2 Seville oranges
3 large carrots, peeled
Small pinch saffron (optional)
1–2 tablesp brown sugar
1 tablesp shredded almonds and/or pistachio nuts

Slice the onions and brown them in oil, then brown the venison. Stir in the cinnamon and add enough water to cover the meat. Cover and simmer for 45 minutes, stirring occasionally so it does not stick to the bottom, and top it up with water if need be.

Meanwhile, peel off the orange zest as thinly as you can. Cut the peel into thin strips, put them into a little pan covered with water, bring to the boil, and drain off the water. Repeat this twice more. This takes the worst bitterness out, leaving them with the right degree of tartness.

Cut the carrots into thin strips and fry them in oil for 15–20 minutes. Add these to the stew with the orange peel strips and the saffron. Squeeze all the juice and any usable flesh from the oranges, discarding the many pips and connecting membrane, and add this to the stew. Continue cooking for another half-hour.

Then taste it and season with salt and pepper. Adjust the sweet/tart flavours with the sugar if needed. Allow everything to simmer for a minute or two, while you shred the almonds and/or pistachios. Scatter these over the dish just before serving with plain rice.

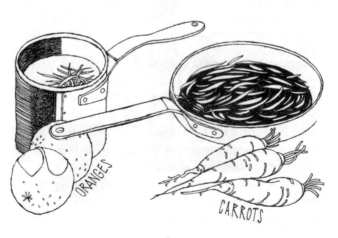

What to serve with venison

Introduction

I am so often asked what to serve with venison. The easy answer is 'anything that goes with beef' – and indeed horse-radish sauce goes very well with venison steaks and roast. Because venison is so lean, it is important to consider texture as well as flavour, especially when it is being cooked through, as in stews or mince. Below are some flavour- and texture-pairings for venison, plus guidance on how to make really good sauces. I've added a few of my favourite recipes. Classics such as braised red cabbage, rösti potatoes, gratin dauphinoise, hollandaise and béarnaise sauces, rowan and redcurrant jellies all go brilliantly with venison and can be found easily on the internet or in my other books.

Flavour pairings
Aromatic: juniper, gin, saffron
Sweet: honey, brandy, whisky, wine
Fruity: apricot, bramble (blackberry), orange, plum, prune, raspberry, redcurrant, rowan

Spicy: clove, fennel, ginger, horseradish, mustard, nutmeg, star anise

Herb: parsley, coriander, fennel, lovage, rosemary, tarragon, thyme

Vegetable: celery, celeriac, courgette, carrot, bulb fennel, mushroom, red cabbage, spinach

Complementary textures

Egg-based sauces: e.g. hollandaise, béarnaise

Syrupy sauces: e.g. *jus*, *demiglace*, red wine sauce

Creamy sauces: e.g. béchamel-based, cream/sour cream, cheese and gratins of vegetables

Vegetables: aubergine, carrot, courgette, mushroom, parsnip, peppers, onion

Starches: cooked pearl barley, gratin dauphinoise, hasselback, roast, sauté or rösti potatoes

Fruit: apricot, prune, orange

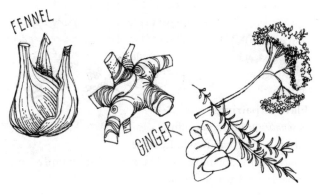

Clear sauces

The basis of the classic clear sauce is *jus,* which is the cooking juices of roast meat, or *demiglace*, which is reduced stock (see p.88). Reduced meat stock becomes a syrupy base to which other flavours, or simply seasoning, can be added. It is always better to have just a small amount of something concentrated than a lot of watery liquid. Adding wine, orange juice, vegetable or fruit purées, or a dash of cream will all give a simple but delicious sauce that only needs boiling to concentrate it, and seasoning. For a thicker sauce, you can make a roux (butter and flour cooked together) and add stock instead of milk.

Creamy sauces

The texture of creamy sauces made from butter and cream complement venison perfectly, even if they do negate its low-fat advantage. Blue cheese melted in cream and the pan- or roasting-juices is a favourite. Egg- and butter-based sauces like hollandaise and béarnaise are brilliant with steaks and roasts. And vegetables served in a smooth cheese sauce make a delightful accompaniment. A flour-based sauce will also make a good texture contrast.

36. Greenmantle sauce

This is an example of a creamy sauce that doesn't use much (if any) cream. It's delicious with roasts or steaks, or poured over leeks to serve with a casserole, or even diluted further into a soup. I like it because it makes use of parts you'd normally throw away. The green part is usually about half the weight of bought leeks.

Serves 4–6
150g (5oz) green tops of leeks
30g (1oz) butter
3 tablesp flour
300ml (½ pint) milk or cream

Chop the leeks into pieces and wash them in a large bowl of cold water so any grit sinks to the bottom. Lift out the leeks and boil them in a small amount of water till tender. Blitz in a food processor or blender – you should get about 300ml (½ pint). Melt the butter in a saucepan and stir in the flour. Add the puréed leeks gradually, beating out any lumps that form. Cook gently for 5–10 minutes so the flour is cooked, topping up with milk, cream or water if it gets too thick. Season to taste.

37. Good venison stock and *demiglace*

Stock is great for making soup, while *demiglace* makes the best sauces ever. Make a batch of stock once or twice a year and boil it right down, then freeze it in tiny pots or ice cube trays. Having this treasure in your freezer means you can always make a reliable sauce, as explained above.

For flavour, use really meaty bones and meat scraps, then add bones with cartilage to give a silky texture. Store bones and meat scraps in the freezer until you have enough. If you order bones from a butcher, ask for some knuckle bones, explain what they are for, and get them cut small enough to fit your largest pot. Three kg (6½lbs) will cover a roasting tin. Chopped onions, celery and carrots intensify the flavour.

Spread out the meat scraps and bones in a roasting tray and brush with oil. Roast or grill, turning occasionally until they are dark brown all over, but not black, as this makes stock bitter. Then tip everything into a large pot and cover with water. Make sure to dissolve all the brownings left on the roasting tray. Simmer for 3–4 hrs, then strain it through a fine sieve or cloth and let it cool. Skim off any fat on the surface. This stock is good for soup or stews. To make *demiglace*, return the stock to a clean pan and boil hard until it has reduced to a quarter of its volume. Don't season it. When cold it is a jelly.

38. Clear red wine sauce

Serves 4–6
200ml (7 fl. oz) venison *demiglace* (see p.88)
120ml (4 fl. oz) red wine
12 crushed juniper berries
1–2 tablesp redcurrant or rowan jelly

Simmer the wine and stock gently together with the juniper berries for 10 minutes so their flavour is extracted. Add some water if it starts to go sticky (you can always boil it down again). Then strain off the juniper berries, as they are very strong. Add jelly to taste and boil until it is a clear, syrupy sauce. Season to taste.

CASSEROLE

RED WINE

39. Pickled blackberries

Excellent with steaks or roasts as a relish, or with cold or smoked venison. They keep almost indefinitely and the extra juice can be used for sauces. You can substitute damsons or even peeled and quartered pears, though the pears may take longer to cook.

200g (7oz) blackberries
100ml (3½ fl. oz) cider vinegar
150g (5½oz) caster sugar
½ teasp ginger
¼ teasp allspice
¼ teasp cinnamon
⅛ teasp cloves
2 cardamom pods, crushed

Put everything except the vinegar into a bowl and mix together. Leave overnight. Next day bring the vinegar to a slow boil, add the blackberry/spice mix and simmer for 10–15 minutes. Put into a hot sterilised jar and seal.

40. Celeriac strudel

This recipe was the star of one of my many cooking demonstrations at the Scone game fair; it goes brilliantly with steaks, roasts or stews.

Serves 4

200g (7oz) diced celeriac
1 small onion, chopped
1 clove garlic, crushed
200g (7oz) butter puff pastry
Handful parsley, finely chopped
2 tablesp finely chopped fresh lovage, or fennel
60g (2oz) grated cheese
1 egg, beaten
1 teasp dried fennel seeds (optional)

Preheat the oven to 200°C (400°F, Gas 6). Boil the celeriac – it cooks quickly – then drain and lightly crush it. Soften the onion and garlic in a little oil and mix them into the cooked celeriac.

Roll out the pastry very thinly and spread the celeriac/onion mixture on top, leaving a generous border round the edge for sealing it. Sprinkle the fresh herbs and cheese over the celeriac, season with salt and pepper, then roll it up, being careful not to break the pastry. Place it carefully onto a baking sheet, using a broad fish slice to transfer it if necessary. Then brush with beaten egg and scatter the fennel seeds on top. Bake for about 20 minutes until the pastry is pale gold, then turn the oven down to 180°C (350°F, Gas 4) and cook for a further 15–20 minutes to allow it to cook through.

41. Black pudding and parsnip galettes

Great with roasts, steaks or stews, this recipe is also good using haggis instead of black pudding.

Serves 4
8 parsnips
250g (9oz) black pudding
Butter and olive oil
Fresh thyme

Preheat the oven to 180°C (350°F, Gas 4). Peel the parsnips and slice into very thin discs. Butter a flat ovenproof tin and, using half of the slices, make four rounds of overlapping circles about 10cm (4in.) in diameter. Remove the skin from the black pudding and divide it into four. Press it out till it more or less covers the parsnips and place on top. Then cover with the remaining parsnip discs, overlapping them again. Place a thin slab of butter on top of each one, and then put the tray into the oven. Keep an eye on them while cooking and if they start to curl up, press them down gently. Once nicely golden brown, turn them over with a fish slice and cook the other side. The whole process takes 20–30 minutes, depending on the thickness of the slices.

42. Courgette fritters

The creamy texture and bright, zingy flavour is perfect for venison in the summertime. This mixture is quite soft and therefore slightly messy to coat in flour before cooking, so it's important to drain the courgettes thoroughly – it takes a good hour to squeeze as much water out as possible. You can play around with the ingredients, especially the herbs.

Makes 10–12 fritters
2 medium courgettes
1 dessertsp salt
3 spring onions or small shallots, finely chopped
125g (4oz) grated feta or mozzarella cheese
Zest of 1–2 limes or 1 lemon
75g (3oz) flour
2 teasp sweet paprika
Handful of fresh herbs (mint, coriander, chervil, etc.), finely chopped
1 huge egg, beaten
Flour or breadcrumbs for dusting (or use egg and breadcrumbs)

Grate the courgettes coarsely, sprinkle with the salt, then put them in a sieve over a bowl. Place another bowl containing a heavy tin in the sieve to press the courgettes and drain out as much water as possible for about an hour. Halfway through, pack the sides to the middle so it all gets pressed.

Mix the spring onion, cheese, zest, flour and paprika

together, and then stir in the herbs, courgette and finally the egg. Form fritters with a spoon and briefly coat each side with flour before frying them gently in a mixture of butter and oil. Don't make them too thick or they won't cook through before the outside burns.

43. Hasselback potatoes

Everybody adores these – the end result looks far more clever than it really is. The exact timing depends on the size of the potatoes but if you allow 1½ hours to prepare and cook them, they will happily keep warm for a while if they are ready sooner than that.

Preheat the oven to 200° C (400°F, Gas 6). Scrub the potatoes thoroughly. Sit a potato in the cup of a wooden spoon (this prevents you from slicing right through the potato). Then, with a sharp knife, make cuts about 5mm (¼ in.) wide all the way down, as though you were partially slicing a loaf of bread. Continue with the rest of the potatoes. Smear a small knob of butter onto each potato and drizzle them all with a little oil, then sprinkle with salt and ground pepper. Bake for about ¾–1 hour, depending on size. After about half an hour, baste the potatoes with the buttery oil. When done, the potatoes will have opened out slightly, like a fan, crisp on top and moist and creamy in the centre.

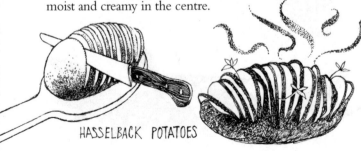

HASSELBACK POTATOES